ROSH HASHANAH

By
Shalini Vallepur

©2021
BookLife Publishing Ltd.
King's Lynn
Norfolk, PE30 4LS

All rights reserved.
Printed in Malta.

A catalogue record for this book is available from the British Library.

ISBN: 978-1-83927-471-8

Written by:
Shalini Vallepur

Edited by:
Madeline Tyler

Designed by:
Drue Rintoul

All facts, statistics, web addresses and URLs in this book were verified as valid and accurate at time of writing. No responsibility for any changes to external websites or references can be accepted by either the author or publisher.

Photo Credits

All images are courtesy of Shutterstock.com. With thanks to Getty Images, Thinkstock Photo and iStockphoto.
Front Cover – Gelpi. 2–3 – Natalia Van Doninck. 4–5 – Gelpi, tomertu, Noam Armonn. 6–7 – Roman Yanushevsky, William Cushman. 8–9 – Roman Yanushevsky, Inna Reznik. 10–11 – Maglara, Amanita Silvicora, Dragana Eric, VectorShow. 12–13 – Africa Studio, David Cohen 156. 14–15 – Amateur007, DCrane, MIA Studio. 16–17 – Gil Cohen Magen, Dr. Avishai Dr. Avishai Teicher Pikiwiki Israel / CC BY. 18–19 – ungvar, avishag shuva. 20–21 – LCRP, Monkey Business Images. 22–23 – McCormick French, Gelpi.

CONTENTS

Page 4	Celebrate Rosh Hashanah with Me!
Page 6	Judaism
Page 8	Rosh Hashanah
Page 10	The Story of Rosh Hashanah
Page 12	Rosh Hashanah Services
Page 14	The Shofar
Page 16	Tashlich
Page 18	Lighting Candles
Page 20	Festive Food
Page 22	Rosh Hashanah around the World
Page 24	Glossary and Index

Words that look like this can be found in the glossary on page 24.

Celebrate Rosh Hashanah with Me!

Shana Tovah! That means 'good year' in Hebrew. My name is David and I will tell you about Rosh Hashanah.

Rosh Hashanah is a festival where lots of families in the Jewish <u>community</u> come together. Come and celebrate with me!

Rosh Hashanah means 'head of the year' and is also known as the Jewish New Year.

JUDAISM

Rosh Hashanah is a festival that is part of a religion called Judaism. Judaism began around 4,000 years ago in the Middle East. We believe that there is one God.

The Star of David is a Jewish symbol.

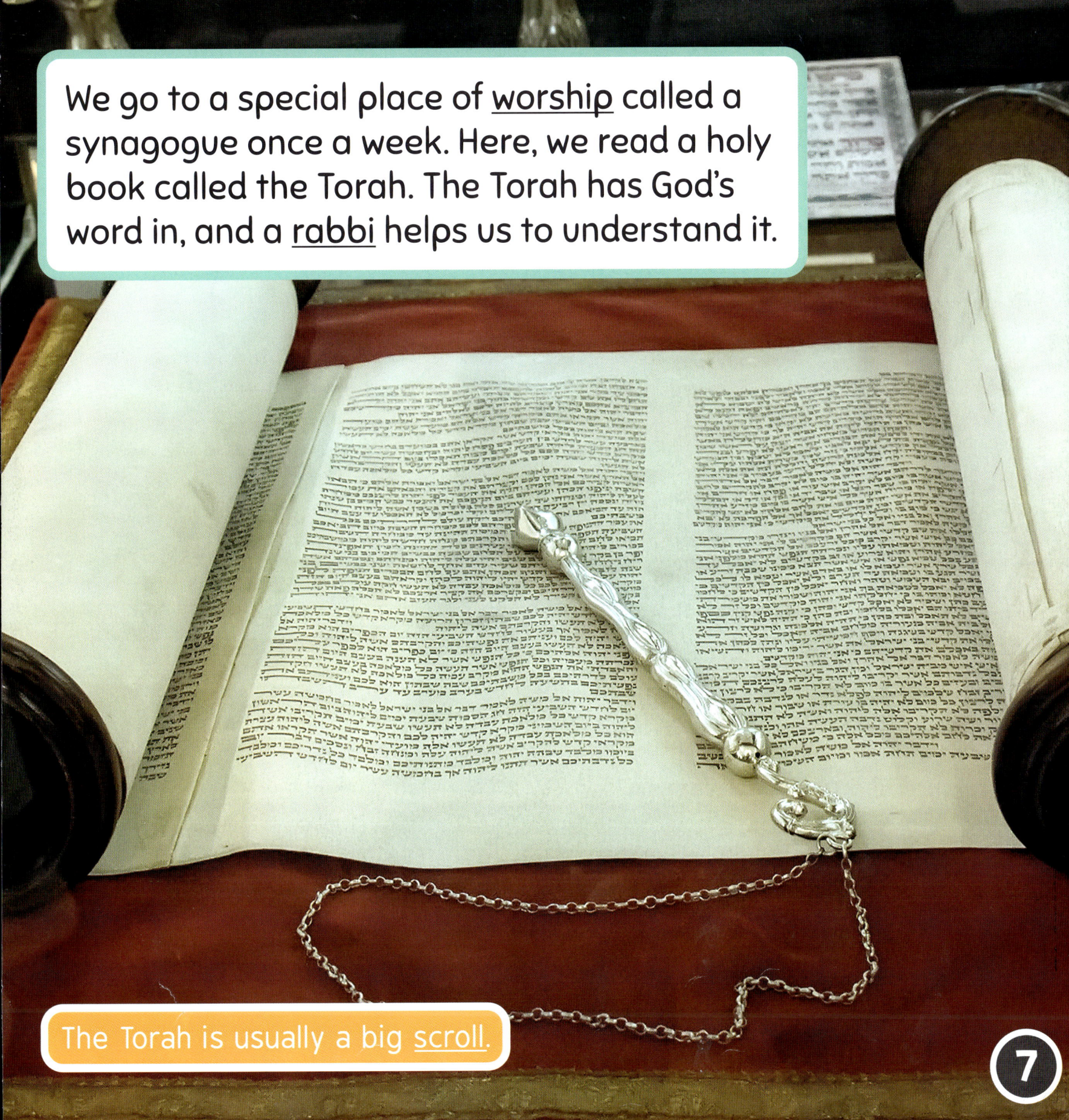

We go to a special place of <u>worship</u> called a synagogue once a week. Here, we read a holy book called the Torah. The Torah has God's word in, and a <u>rabbi</u> helps us to understand it.

The Torah is usually a big <u>scroll</u>.

ROSH HASHANAH

We celebrate Rosh Hashanah on the first two days of Tishrei. Tishrei is the seventh month of the Hebrew calendar.

Rosh Hashanah usually happens around the end of September or the start of October.

Torah

Shofar

Rosh Hashanah is a happy time. It is also a time to think about the year that has passed and about any bad things we have done.

THE STORY OF ROSH HASHANAH

Rosh Hashanah is the Jewish New Year. It is when we celebrate the creation of the world and think about making a fresh start.

We believe that God decides what the next year of our lives will be like during Rosh Hashanah. We can ask God to forgive us if we feel that we have done anything wrong. Many people will think about what is important to them. Some people may think about all the things they want to do in the next year.

Rosh Hashanah Services

Special services take place at the synagogue during Rosh Hashanah. We usually sing hymns and say different types of prayers. Parts of the Torah are read aloud by the rabbi.

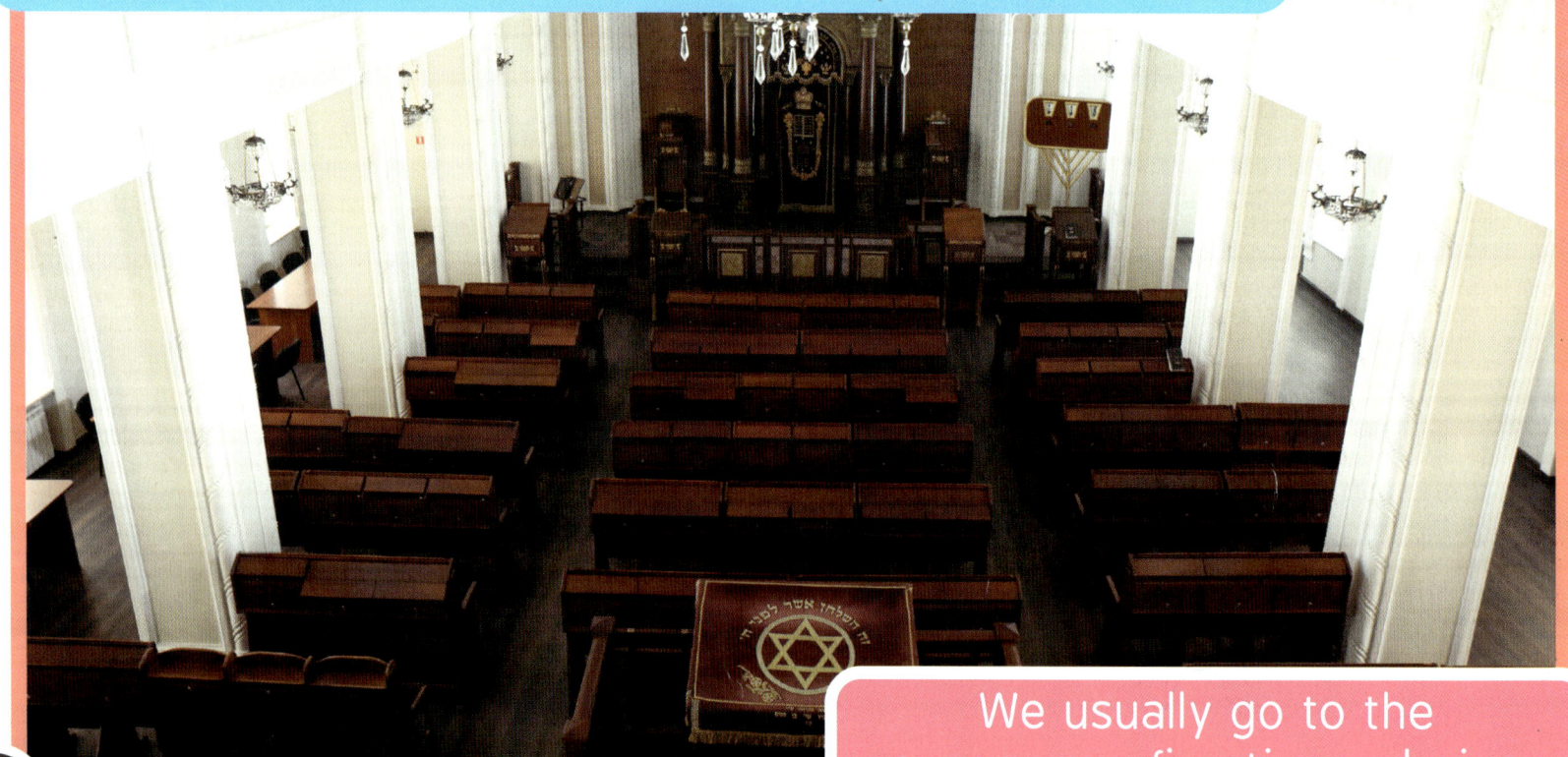

We usually go to the synagogue five times during Rosh Hashanah.

Amidah is the silent prayer. We stand and say it in our heads. We ask God to forgive us when we pray during Rosh Hashanah.

Tallit

Men usually wear a tallit over their shoulders during morning services.

THE SHOFAR

The shofar is blown during morning services of Rosh Hashanah. It makes a loud sound. We believe that it welcomes in the new year.

Ram

The shofar is usually a ram's horn.

There are different types of shofar blasts – some are long and others are short. When we hear the shofar, we think about God, ourselves and the world around us.

The shofar can be blown up to 100 times on each day of Rosh Hashanah.

TASHLICH

Some people may perform tashlich on the first day of Rosh Hashanah. Everybody gathers by running water, such as a river. We say special prayers and may throw breadcrumbs into the water.

If people can't get to a river, they can use a hose.

When we throw the breadcrumbs, we believe we are getting rid of any bad things we may have done. Some people may shake their clothes as well.

As we see and hear the water, we remember God and his word.

LIGHTING CANDLES

Candles are usually lit during Rosh Hashanah. On the first night, we light candles about 18 minutes before sunset.

We say a prayer after the candles are lit.

On the second night, we light more candles. We try to take the flame from a candle that is already burning.

FESTIVE FOOD

Somebody will say a special prayer before we eat. This is called kiddush. Many people eat apples dipped in honey. New fruits are also eaten. These are fruits that have just become ready to eat for the first time that year.

We eat sweet food so that we will have a sweet year!

After kiddush and the new fruits, we eat challah. Challah is a loaf of bread. We usually make round challah during Rosh Hashanah. We sometimes dip it in honey to make it sweet.

ROSH HASHANAH AROUND THE WORLD

Jewish people live all over the world, so there are many Rosh Hashanah celebrations in lots of different countries. Why not see if there is a synagogue in your local area that you could visit to help you learn more?

Synagogue in Liverpool, UK

I hope you have learnt a lot about Rosh Hashanah and understand why and how we celebrate it.

GLOSSARY

community	a group of people who are connected by something
forgive	to stop feeling anger towards someone for something they did
hymns	religious songs or poems in praise of God
rabbi	a teacher of Judaism
scroll	a big roll of paper
services	religious acts of praise to a god or gods, carried out in a particular order
worship	a religious act where a person shows their love for a god

INDEX

candles 18–19
challah 21
Days of Awe 11
fruit 20–21
kiddush 20–21
prayers 12–13, 16, 18, 20

shofar 9, 14–15
synagogues 7, 12, 22
tallits 13
tashlich 16–17
Tishrei 8
Torah 7, 9, 12